My Science Library

How Do Humans Depend on Earth?

by Julie K. Lundgren

Science Content Editor:

Shirley Duke

Rourke
Educational Media

rourkeeducationalmedia.com

Teacher Notes available at
rem4teachers.com

Science Content Editor: Shirley Duke holds a bachelor's degree in biology and a master's degree in education from Austin College in Sherman, Texas. She taught science in Texas at all levels for twenty-five years before starting to write for children. Her science books include *You Can't Wear These Genes, Infections, Infestations, and Diseases, Enterprise STEM, Forces and Motion at Work, Environmental Disasters,* and *Gases.* She continues writing science books and also works as a science content editor.

www.rourkeeducationalmedia.com

Photo credits: Cover © Stephen Mcsweeny; Pages 2/3 © Smileus; Pages 4/5 © Elenamiv, Anton Balazh; Pages 6/7 © liznel, Walter G Arce, Ann Cantelow; Pages 8/9 © Iakov Filimonov, Steve Heap; Pages 10/11 © Scott Bauer, Mikhail Malyshev; Pages 12/13 © snowturtle, buriy, Smileus Pages 14/15 © Grauvision, Ninell, Sergio33, Rudy Umans; Pages 16/17 © NASA, Antonina Potapenko; Pages 18/19 © Piotr Marcinski, Steshkin Yevgeniy, ifong, gallimaufry; Pages 20/21 © Lisovskaya Natalia, MarchCattle

Editor: Kelli Hicks

My Science Library series produced by Blue Door Publishing, Florida for Rourke Educational Media.

Library of Congress PCN Data

Lundgren, Julie K.
 How Do Humans Depend on Earth? / Julie K. Lundgren.
   p. cm. -- (My Science Library)
 ISBN 978-1-61810-105-1 (Hard cover) (alk. paper)
 ISBN 978-1-61810-238-6 (Soft cover)
 Library of Congress Control Number: 2012930303

Rourke Educational Media
Printed in the United States of America,
North Mankato, Minnesota

Rourke
Educational Media

rourkeeducationalmedia.com

customerservice@rourkeeducationalmedia.com
PO Box 643328 Vero Beach, Florida 32964

Table of Contents

Earth Provides

People depend on plants for food, clean air, water, fuel, clothing, and shelter. Nearly all food webs begin with plants, the **primary producers**. During **photosynthesis**, green plants use sunlight to change **carbon dioxide** from the air and water into simple sugars made of carbon, hydrogen, and oxygen. Plants store the sugars in their roots, stems, and leaves. As we eat plants, energy and nutrition pass on to our bodies.

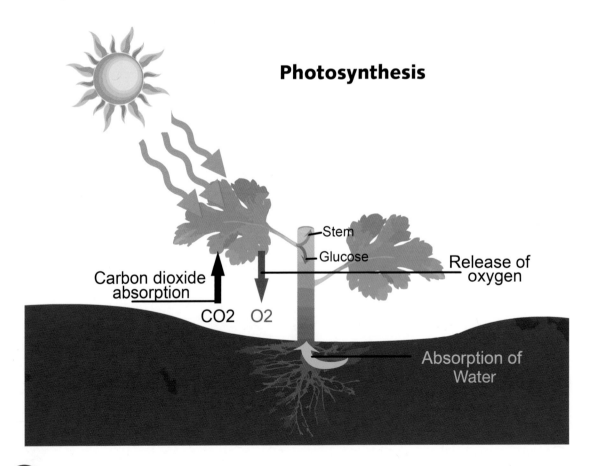

Photosynthesis

Stem

Glucose

Release of oxygen

Carbon dioxide absorption

CO_2 O_2

Absorption of Water

Plants take in carbon dioxide and give off oxygen during photosynthesis. A balance of these gases in our atmosphere keeps Earth's climate stable. Carbon dioxide causes Earth to retain heat. By removing carbon dioxide from the atmosphere and increasing oxygen, plants cool the Earth and provide oxygen for people to breathe.

Since the first land plants began growing 450 to 500 million years ago, Earth's climate and landscape has changed from warm, rocky, and harsh, to cool and green because of the exchange of carbon dioxide and oxygen during photosynthesis.

Plants help purify Earth's water. As wetlands receive and filter water runoff, the reeds, grasses, and other plants remove fertilizers used in farming, trap sediments, and reduce **erosion** and flooding by holding and slowly releasing water.

Trees provide us with lumber for building homes. We produce cloth from the fibers of cotton, flax, bamboo, and other plants.

As our country's population increases, so does its demands for timber.

We use cotton fibers to make denim jeans and dollar bills.

At one time, farmers and builders thought of United States wetlands as wastelands, but now recognize their value as water purifiers and habitats for plants and animals.

From the very beginning, people have gathered wild plants and fruits as food. Groups moved from place to place during the year in order to collect food plants at peak times of availability or ripeness. Later in human history, agriculture became part of many cultures, allowing people to stay in one place instead of moving according to food location.

Home gardens and small farms continue to provide fresh, locally grown food to families and communities. Local farmers provide food seasonally in small quantities.

When corn and eastern gamagrass cross pollinate, agronomists hope that the resulting hybrids will better resist disease, cold weather, and drought.

Advanced technology has changed what and how much farmers grow. Developments include enhanced **hybrid** crops. Two parent plants with different desired characteristics can produce hybrid plants that consistently have both characteristics.

Genetically modified crops introduce a desired quality in plants. Living things have sets of instructions built into their cells. These instructions, or genes, shape what living things look like and how they grow.

When food scientists insert a gene into a plant's set of instructions, they produce genetically modified crops. The genes inserted may make plants resist disease, insects, or **herbicides**.

Concerns about genetically modified crops include **outcrossing**, where a genetically modified crop plant pollinates a traditional crop plant or wild plant relative, introducing the new gene into crops grown for another use or into nature.

From Moo Crew Stew to You

A genetically modified crop grown for cattle may not have been tested for human use, yet it can pollinate human crops and pass on the new gene to our food.

People use plants as fuel for transportation and heat. We burn fossil fuels, the buried, ancient remains of plants and animals found in the form of coal, oil, and natural gas. Fossil fuels store carbon, just as living trees and plants do. When burned, they release carbon dioxide into the air. The large and growing amounts of carbon dioxide in our atmosphere cause Earth's climate to warm.

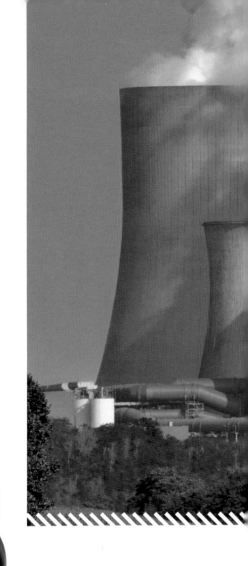

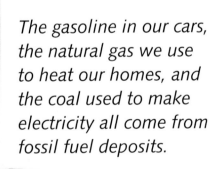

The gasoline in our cars, the natural gas we use to heat our homes, and the coal used to make electricity all come from fossil fuel deposits.

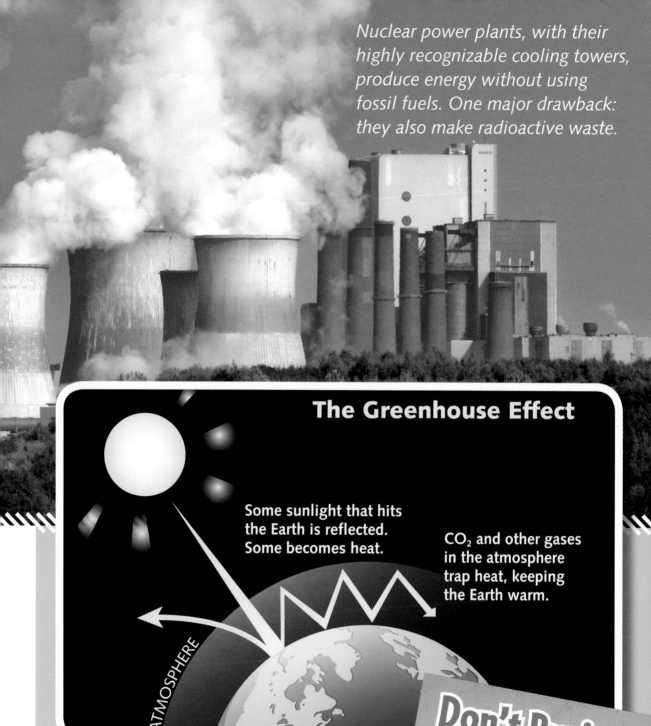

Nuclear power plants, with their highly recognizable cooling towers, produce energy without using fossil fuels. One major drawback: they also make radioactive waste.

The Greenhouse Effect

Some sunlight that hits the Earth is reflected. Some becomes heat.

CO_2 and other gases in the atmosphere trap heat, keeping the Earth warm.

ATMOSPHERE

High in Earth's atmosphere, carbon dioxide (CO_2) acts like a blanket, blocking the escape of heat to outer space. Putting too much carbon dioxide in the air can result in an overall warming of Earth.

Don't Panic Now But...

The last 10 years have been the warmest decade ever recorded in human history.

Measuring Our Impact

Human activities once had little effect on Earth, but today we impact Earth in harmful ways. The world population has soared to 7 billion people. More countries use fossil fuels in ever increasing amounts, causing global climate change, air and water pollution, more trash, and human illness.

If we add up all the ways we contribute to global climate change through the production of carbon dioxide, we come up with a measure scientists call a carbon footprint. When we flip on a light, ride in a car fueled by gasoline, or turn up the heat in our homes, we increase our carbon footprint.

Our carbon footprint also increases when we buy foods from distant places because of the large amount of fuel used to transport it to our local grocery stores.

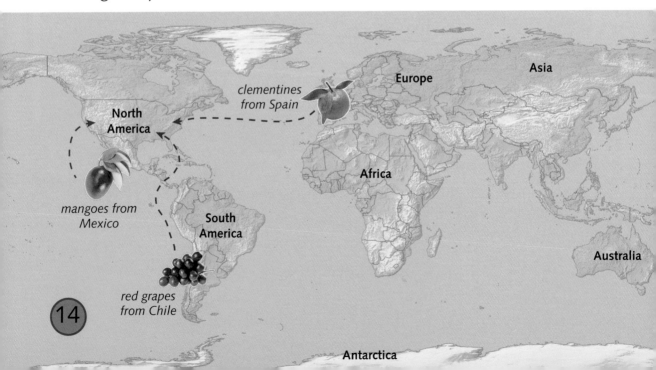

clementines from Spain

Europe

Asia

North America

mangoes from Mexico

Africa

South America

Australia

red grapes from Chile

Antarctica

Pesticides get washed away by rain into nearby streams or groundwater, polluting the large, natural underground stores of water.

A growing population needs more of other resources, too. Large, industrial farms produce much needed food crops, but also add to environmental problems with water contamination by **pesticides**, herbicides, and fertilizer runoff. As more genetically modified crops enter production, outcrossing and other problems may grow. We may not have solutions to these problems yet. What cost do we pay to fix our water and food supplies?

Don't Panic Now But...

Earth has limited resources. **Nonrenewable** resources like fossil fuels will eventually run out. Estimates predict that people will use all available fossil fuels in the next 40 to 70 years.

In countries with high growth and high resource needs, people threaten whole ecosystems. The high demand for lumber and farmland endangers rainforests and other **old growth** forests. Once destroyed, we cannot create these forests again.

Disappearing Forests

Satellites take photographs of Earth's rainforests and scientists use them to estimate the rate and amount of rainforest lost each year. They estimate that 38,600 square miles (100,000 square kilometers) of this nonrenewable resource disappear annually. Farms and towns encroach ever further into the forest.

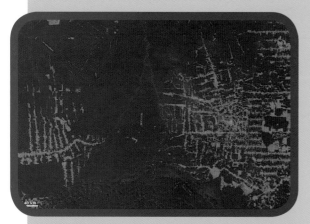

Satellite view of an area of rainforest in Brazil, 2001.

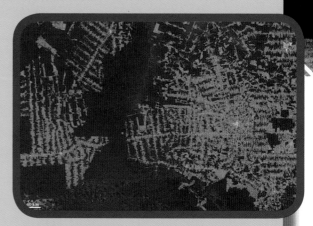

Satellite view of same area of forest, 2010.

The slash and burn method of agriculture opens up forest land for farming, but has several negative effects like erosion, nutrient loss, and habitat loss.

Tropical rainforests hold more than half of Earth's plant species. Continued deforestation will result in the loss of **biodiversity** and its many benefits to our planet. We need these plants to take up carbon dioxide and produce oxygen for a healthy and stable climate.

Green and Clean

Further use and development of renewable resources and **conservation** of both nonrenewable and renewable resources will help the Earth stay healthy and still provide for our needs. By cutting back on actions that contribute to problems, we reduce our carbon footprint. Our garbage landfill use decreases when we recycle, use cloth shopping bags, and **compost** kitchen waste like bread crusts, vegetable peelings, and fruit scraps.

Reducing waste production and recycling all waste that can be recycled lessens the need for landfills.

In many areas, clean water is in short supply. We can reduce our water use by taking shorter showers, fixing dripping faucets, and adding mulch around plants. To reduce evaporation, water lawns and gardens using drip hoses or water during the coolest part of the day.

Growing and buying organic food reduces the amount of pesticides and chemical fertilizers in our water and food. Organic clothing helps, too. Activities that support the Earth also include landscaping with native plants. Once established, these plants grow with little care since they have adaptations for living in that habitat.

Although we may pay a bit more for organic food at the store, we save on paying for costs to fix environmental problems caused by foods produced with pesticides and other chemicals.

NO CHEMICAL SPRAYING

ORGANIC FARM

Pack a Green Lunch

Reducing your carbon footprint can be inconvenient at times, but you can easily pack a green lunch. Instead of a paper bag and napkin, choose a reusable, insulated lunch bag and cloth napkin. Use reusable containers instead of plastic bags and throwaway packaging. Pour a cold drink into a thermos and toss in an organic apple to finish your feast.

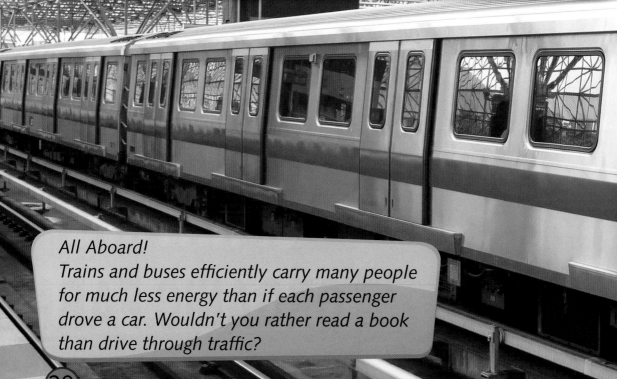

All Aboard!
Trains and buses efficiently carry many people for much less energy than if each passenger drove a car. Wouldn't you rather read a book than drive through traffic?

Carpooling, biking, and using public transportation like trains and buses reduce our carbon footprint, too. Substituting renewable, clean fuels made from plants instead of fossil fuels produces less air pollution. We can buy gasoline blended with ethanol, a renewable fuel made from corn or sugar cane.

A clean, healthy Earth with abundant biodiversity and a stable climate can provide well for human needs. Responsible actions by every person everyday make a difference.

Show What You Know

1. How do plants help shape Earth's climate?

2. Some fossil fuel deposits lie under unspoiled natural areas. As we use up resources in other places, should we sacrifice these nature reserves? Why or why not?

3. In what ways can you reduce your carbon footprint?

Glossary

biodiversity (bye-oh-duh-VERS-it-tee): the number of different kinds of life in a habitat or place

carbon dioxide (KAR-buhn die-OK-side): a colorless, odorless gas produced by plant and fossil fuel combustion and a major cause of global climate change

compost (KOM-pohst): to allow the decomposition of plant based food and yard waste, like grass clippings and vegetable peels

conservation (kon-sur-VAY-shuhn): the protection and careful and wise use of resources, so as to preserve them for the future

erosion (ih-ROH-zhuhn): the loss of topsoil and with it, the essential nutrients for growing plants

herbicides (HER-buh-sydz): chemicals people use to kill unwanted plants or weeds

hybrid (HYE-brid): the offspring resulting from a cross between two varieties of a plant or closely related plants

nonrenewable (non-ri-NOO-uh-buhl): limited, and permanently gone when used

old growth (OHLD GROHTH): original, never before disturbed by humans

outcrossing (OUT-krawss-ing): reproduction between a genetically modified plant and a traditional crop or wild plant

pesticides (PESS-tuh-sydz): chemicals that kill insects and other pests, especially those that eat farm crops

Index

Websites to Visit

http://climate.nasa.gov/warmingworld/

http://epa.gov/climatechange/kids/index.html

www.meetthegreens.org/

About the Author

Julie K. Lundgren has written more than 40 nonfiction books for children. She gets a kick out of sharing juicy facts about science, nature, and animals, especially if they are slightly disgusting! Through her work, she hopes kids will learn that Earth is an amazing place and young people can make a big difference in keeping our planet healthy. She lives in Minnesota with her family.

Ask The Author!
www.rem4students.com